WHAT'S THE DEAL?

Ecstasy

K

www.heinemann.co.uk/library
Visit our website to find out more information about Heinemann Library books.

To order:
 Phone 44 (0) 1865 888066
Send a fax to 44 (0) 1865 314091
 Visit the Heinemann Bookshop at www.heinemann.co.uk/library to browse
our catalogue and order online.

Produced for Heinemann Library by
White-Thomson Publishing Ltd,
Bridgewater Business Centre,
210 High Street, Lewes,
East Sussex, BN7 2NH.

First published in Great Britain by Heinemann Library,
Jordan Hill, Oxford OX2 8EJ, part of Harcourt Education.

Heinemann Library is a registered trademark of
Harcourt Education Ltd.

Consultant: Jenny McWhirter, Head of Education and
    Prevention, DrugScope
Editorial: Clare Collinson
Design: Tim Mayer
Picture Research: Amy Sparks
Production: Duncan Gilbert

Originated by P.T. Repro Multi Warna
Printed and bound in China, by South China
    Printing Company.

The paper used to print this book comes from
sustainable resources.

The case studies and quotations in this book are
based on factual examples. However, in some cases,
the names or other personal information have been
changed to protect the privacy of the individual
concerned.

10 digit ISBN 0 431 10776 9 (hardback)
13 digit ISBN 978 0 431 10776 9 (hardback)
10 09 08 07 06
10 9 8 7 6 5 4 3 2 1

10 digit ISBN 0 431 10788 2 (paperback)
13 digit ISBN 978 0 431 10788 2 (paperback)
11 10 09 08 07
10 9 8 7 6 5 4 3 2 1

British Library Cataloguing in Publication Data
Fitzhugh, Karla
    Ecstasy. – (What's the deal?)
    1. Ecstasy (Drug) – Juvenile literature
    I. Title
    362.2'99
A full catalogue record for this book is available from
the British Library.

Acknowledgements
The publisher would like to thank the following for
their kind permission to use their photographs:

Alamy 10 (Henry Westheim), 14–15 (Photofusion
Picture Library), 25 (Houston Scott/Corbis Sygma), 32
(Bob Pardue), 35 (Medical-on-Line), 38 (Bob Jones
Photography), 47 (Photo Network); Corbis 8 (Peter
Beck), 11 (Scott Houston), 16 (RNT Productions), 26
(Houston Scott/Corbis Sygma), 28–29 (Pete Saloutos),
36–37 (Steve Prezant), 49 (Ed Bock), 50–51 (Gabe
Palmer); Getty Images 4–5 (Stone), 9 (The Image
Bank), 13 (Stone), 17 (Taxi), 20 (The Image Bank), 23
(Stone), 40 (Taxi), 41 (Stone), 42 (Stone), 44 (Taxi), 45
(Stone), 48 (Stone); Rex Features 7 (Sakki), 18–19
(TS/Keystone), 30 (Garo/Phanie), 34 (IPC Magazines:
Chat), 43 (Greg Mathieson); Science Photo Library 21
(Victor de Schwanberg), 33 (St Bartholomew's
Hospital); Topfoto/Image Works 46.

Cover artwork by Phil Weyman, Kralinator Design.

Every effort has been made to contact copyright
holders of any material reproduced in this book. Any
omissions will be rectified in subsequent printings if
notice is given to the publishers.

R0002655 · 11·11

Contents

❚ Words appearing in the text in bold, **like this**, are explained in the Glossary.

When people are offered ecstasy, they are often told that it is completely safe and they will have a great time. Sarah tried ecstasy for the first time in her early teens, and is now suffering from the after-effects.

"When I was twelve, I wanted to break free from my family and their rules. I guess I was trying to rebel. I hung out in places my parents told me not to go and I guess I got in with a bad crowd. We drank alcohol and smoked, and I started

trying other drugs like speed and cannabis. I was thirteen when I tried ecstasy for the first time. It was like I didn't have a care in the world, at least until I started coming down.

"After partying every weekend for a while, one pill wasn't enough. No matter how many pills I took, I never got the same feeling I had from the first one. When ecstasy wears off, it's the worst feeling ever. I was cranky and tired, and found myself bursting into tears for no reason. I was taking six or seven pills every weekend, and getting really messed up.

"I let it wreck my health, and to this day I don't know why I didn't stop sooner. I hurt my family so much and told so many lies, but at the time I couldn't care less how worried they were. I haven't taken ecstasy for three years now, but I get depressed very easily and my memory is shot to bits. I have so many regrets."

Taking ecstasy has all kinds of risks, and every year many people end up being taken to hospital emergency departments after using this drug. Some people have even died, and it's impossible to predict who will be harmed. As doctors find out more about the effects of ecstasy, there is growing evidence to suggest it can damage the brain and lead to mental health problems.

Making decisions

One day you may be offered ecstasy by someone you know. Do you know what you would say? This book will give you the information you need to make your own decisions about ecstasy. There are many issues to think about. Why do some people use ecstasy and what harm can the drug do to a person's body and mind? Is ecstasy **addictive** and what are the wider effects of ecstasy **abuse**? Get ready to find out – what's the deal with ecstasy?

▌ A person's friends can be a big influence on whether they decide to try drugs or avoid them.

Ecstasy is a **stimulant** drug that speeds up some of the actions of the brain, making people feel as if they have more energy. It is also a mild **hallucinogen** that distorts the way a person sees and feels the things around them.

MDMA

Ecstasy is the street name for a **synthetic** drug called **MDMA**, which is short for "3,4-methylenedioxymethamphetamine". MDMA is just one of a large family of chemicals called **MDA-type drugs** (MDA is short for "3,4-methylenedioxyamphetamine"). Many MDA-type chemicals have effects that are nearly the same as MDMA, and they may be sold illegally as "ecstasy".

What are stimulants?

Stimulants are drugs that speed up the activity in the brain, which affects a person's feelings and thoughts, and other processes in the rest of the body. There are many different types of stimulant drugs. Some, such as caffeine (found in coffee, tea, and some soft drinks), have mild effects. Stronger stimulants include ecstasy, **amphetamines** (also called "speed"), cocaine, and crack.

Stimulant drugs tend to make people feel more energetic, alert, and awake. They also tend to make people feel less hungry. In large amounts stimulants can make people feel jittery and unable to relax or sleep.

Street names for ecstasy

Street names for ecstasy include: adam, bean, disco biscuits, E, eckies, essence, hug drug, love drug, M and Ms, New Yorkers, pills, rolls, sweeties, X, and XTC. Sometimes the name comes from the picture on the pill, such as "doves" or "tulips".

A mild hallucinogen

Ecstasy also has mild hallucinogenic effects. Hallucinogens are drugs that make people have **hallucinations** – they start to feel, see, or hear things that aren't really there. **LSD** or "acid" is another example of a hallucinogen. The hallucinogenic effects of ecstasy are not as strong as those of LSD. With ecstasy, it's rare for users to see things that aren't there, but the drug can increase a person's sense of colour and sound. It can also affect the way they feel about things and make physical sensations seem different.

What does ecstasy look like?

Pure MDMA is a white powder made up of tiny crystals. When it's sold illegally, ecstasy is usually mixed with other ingredients and pressed into the shape of pills. These can be plain or speckled, and may be white or coloured. Sometimes ecstasy pills have a picture or logo stamped on to them. Ecstasy may also be sold as small capsules or as an off-white powder.

▌ Ecstasy pills may look as harmless as sweets, but taking ecstasy has serious health risks.

Ecstasy and the brain

When a person takes ecstasy, the drug is carried to their brain in the bloodstream. Once it enters the brain, the drug causes a massive abnormal release of "messenger" chemicals, such as **serotonin**. The raised levels of these chemicals affect the nerve cells in the brain, making them more active. This causes changes in the person's feelings, senses, moods, and thoughts. They may feel exhilarated and confident and experience a sense of closeness and **empathy** towards those around them.

The changes in the balance of the chemicals in the brain also lead to physical changes in the body, including raised body temperature, increased heart rate, and raised **blood pressure**.

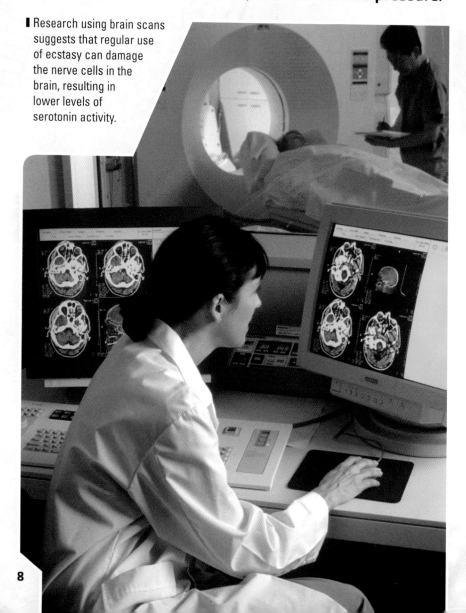

❙ Research using brain scans suggests that regular use of ecstasy can damage the nerve cells in the brain, resulting in lower levels of serotonin activity.

After taking ecstasy, many people say they suffer from tiredness and have difficulty concentrating.

> "A year or more of ecstasy use has affected my son's ability to concentrate and remember things, and made his insecurity worse. We're all wondering if things will ever be the same again."
>
> Cheryl, mother of sixteen-year-old Anthony

Nerve damage

Scientists don't know everything there is to know about serotonin, and there is a lot of research going on to find out more about it. It seems to be important for the control of moods, emotions, and eating and sleeping patterns. Taking ecstasy seems to damage the nerve cells in the brain that make serotonin. Some scientists think that this nerve damage could be permanent. This could badly affect someone's mental and physical health for the rest of their life.

The comedown

By the time the effects of ecstasy have begun to wear off, the amount of messenger chemicals in some parts of the brain have dropped to very low levels. This is because they have been used up quickly, and the body takes time to replace them. This leaves the user feeling tired and irritable, and it can take a few days before they feel normal again. You can read more about these effects, sometimes called a "**comedown**", on pages 24–25.

A delicate balance

The brain is a very sensitive organ, and even tiny changes in the way it works can cause long-lasting changes in a person's thoughts, moods, and feelings. The brain also controls some of the basic functions that keep us all alive, such as regulating body temperature, breathing, and heart rate. A small change in any of these basic functions can make a huge difference to someone's overall health. It could make them seriously ill, or even kill them.

Ecstasy and medical experiments

MDMA, which we now know as ecstasy, was first made by chemists around a hundred years ago. Scientists have carried out a series of experiments to see if the drug might be useful, but it has no approved medical uses in most countries.

Early experiments

MDMA was first made by German scientists in 1912. They were trying to develop drugs for medical purposes. MDMA didn't seem to be useful in treating any diseases, however, so it was ignored for many years. In 1939, researchers started studying MDMA to see if it would work as a drug that could reduce feelings of hunger, and help with weight loss. It was also tested to see if it could help people cope better with stress. These experiments stopped when the Second World War broke out later that year.

Military experiments

In the 1950s, military scientists and governments started testing all kinds of drugs to see if they would be useful during warfare. They hoped to find some drugs that would make soldiers into better fighters, or make enemy spies tell them their secrets. MDMA and other **MDA-type drugs** were tested, but they did not have the effects the scientists were hoping for.

▌Medical experiments with ecstasy are very rare nowadays, and researchers need to follow strict safety rules.

■ The chemist Alexander Shulgin began researching MDMA in the 1970s, hoping it could be used to help people overcome emotional and mental problems.

The 1970s

In the 1970s, a US chemist in California called Alexander Shulgin started looking at MDMA and MDA-type drugs. He made large amounts of these drugs, and experimented with them on himself. Shulgin had a general interest in drugs that affected how the mind worked, and was also looking for drugs that might help people who had **psychological** problems.

A few doctors and therapists in the 1970s thought that giving MDMA to arguing couples during marriage **counselling** might help them to understand one another better. They hoped that the drug would help each person see the point of view of their partner, so they could work through their personal difficulties more easily. However, this did not seem to have much success.

Medical experiments today

Nowadays, MDMA is not used for medical purposes, apart from by a small number of therapists in Switzerland. However, it is sometimes used in carefully controlled medical experiments. To use MDMA in an experiment now, scientists must get a special licence.

A small number of people in the United States used **MDMA** in the 1970s, but by the end of the 1980s its use had spread around the world as part of the dance music scene. People were now calling it "ecstasy".

California in the 1970s

After reading the research of Alexander Shulgin and others, a few people in California began to use MDMA. The drug was mostly taken at very quiet and relaxed parties in somebody's home, where **hippies** and other people sat around and talked. However, most people were not aware of the drug, and it was not widely used.

The house music scene

In the 1980s, this pattern of use changed. In the early 1980s, DJs in nightclubs such as the Warehouse in Chicago, United States, played and mixed old disco records for the crowd, and started using drum machines to make beats. This electronic dance music became known as "warehouse" or "house" music. By the middle of the 1980s, this music dominated the club scene in the United States.

At the same time, drug **dealers** started calling MDMA "ecstasy" and began to sell it to club-goers. The drug appealed to some club-goers because they thought it would give them the energy to dance all night and improve their ability to appreciate the rhythmic sounds of the music. Most people were not aware of the risks of the drug.

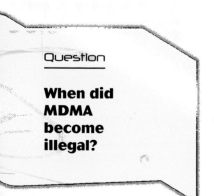

Question

When did MDMA become illegal?

Ecstasy around the world

Ecstasy use spread to Europe in the middle of the 1980s, again linked with hippy culture and the dance music scene. The island of Ibiza, off the coast of Spain, was a hippy hang-out, and a holiday island for wealthy people. The island developed its own version of house music, and many new nightclubs opened for all-night parties or "**raves**". DJs in the United Kingdom were influenced by the Ibiza party scene, and by the music from Chicago. In the United

▌House music began in the 1980s, and has evolved into many forms of dance music that are popular today.

Kingdom in the late 1980s, ecstasy became associated with raves that were organized secretly, mostly outdoors or in warehouses. The police used strong measures to stop these parties and arrest drug dealers. Around the world, ecstasy gradually moved from the dance scene and big cities into other areas, including universities.

Answer

MDMA became illegal in 1977 in the United Kingdom, in 1985 in the United States, and in 1986 in Australia.

Although ecstasy remains popular among some young people, especially those who are part of the club scene, the majority of young people never take ecstasy. Recent surveys suggest that ecstasy use may be decreasing.

Patterns of ecstasy use

Reports in some newspapers sometimes make it look as if all young people are taking ecstasy regularly, but the truth is quite different. Teenagers who try ecstasy are outnumbered by those who decide to avoid it. Out of the small group who do try the drug, most do not take it over a long period, or regularly. They try it a few times and then stop.

Very few people take ecstasy once a week or more, or for many years.

! Ecstasy use today

- In England and Wales, the number of people aged 16 and over who had tried ecstasy increased from 4 per cent in 1998 to 6 per cent in 2001, but has decreased every year since then.

- In the United States in 2002, about 7 per cent of 12th graders (aged about 17) had tried ecstasy at least once. However, since 2002, there has been a drop each year in the number of young people who have taken ecstasy.

People who try ecstasy are most likely to be in their late teens or early twenties, although they may be much younger. Males are slightly more likely to try ecstasy than females. Generally, ecstasy use increased during the 1990s, and then started to decrease.

▌ Some people take ecstasy at home, but the drug is still mainly associated with people who go to dance clubs.

Viewpoints

Some people think that fewer teenagers would try ecstasy if they were educated about drugs at a younger age. Others strongly disagree.

● **Drugs education at an early age helps young people make wiser decisions**
Some ecstasy **dealers** target children at a very young age, so children have to be properly prepared for how they are going to react to this situation. They have to understand the risks of these drugs, and knowing the facts will help give them the confidence to say no.

● **Drugs education introduces young people to drugs too soon**
Educating people at a young age about drugs might make them curious about the drugs and their effects. This could lead to them experimenting with the drugs at a young age. Children should not be told about drugs when they are not old enough to understand about them. It's better just to say that drugs are dangerous and illegal.

What do you think?

Most young people choose not to take ecstasy, but what is it that influences the people who do decide to take it? Sometimes people may be influenced by the behaviour of friends, or by the things they say. When people are offered ecstasy, they are often told that the drug is completely safe and they will have a great time. The truth is that ecstasy has all kinds of risks.

Joining in?

Our friends, classmates, and relatives can have a great influence over us, even if we're not fully aware of it. Most people have a desire to fit in with their friends, and may copy their behaviour as part of this. Although teenagers like to express their individuality, they also want to feel part of a group. They may be at a party or at a dance club where ecstasy is being passed around. They may think if they don't join in, they will start to lose their friends. In a situation like this, it's important to remember that everyone should feel free to make their own decisions.

▌Young people make lots of decisions for themselves. Most young people decide to avoid taking ecstasy, and real friends are supportive of their choice.

Sometimes people tease their friends, or try to persuade them that it's cool to take drugs. They might give bad advice or say that the other person is missing out on having a good time. This pressure, sometimes called "peer pressure" or "peer influence", can be very hard to cope with. There are some ideas for dealing with peer pressure on page 50.

Other influences

A few people may start taking ecstasy every time they go out to parties, because they wrongly believe that it's the only way to have a good time. Other people take ecstasy because they think it will provide a temporary escape from bad feelings, although they can end up feeling worse in the long run. Some people who are shy or lack confidence may be tempted to take ecstasy in social situations, hoping it will make them more outgoing.

Dealer pressure

Many young people face the experience of being offered ecstasy by a **dealer**. Dealers can seem very friendly and persuasive. In situations like this, it can take a lot of confidence simply to say no. However, if a dealer sees that you are really not interested, they will soon stop bothering you.

▌ Drug dealers are out to make money, so sometimes they give bad advice to people to persuade them to buy ecstasy or other drugs.

17

Ecstasy is made illegally in small secret factories or laboratories. It is then smuggled to different countries, and distributed to users through a network of **dealers**. Many ecstasy users obtain the drug from friends or other people they know.

Where is ecstasy made?

Small, illegal ecstasy laboratories exist all over the world, but the drug is produced in large amounts in a number of different countries, including the Netherlands and Belgium in Europe. These illegal labs are not like the hygienic laboratories where medical drugs are made legally. They are often very dirty, and there are no proper safety precautions. They can be set up almost anywhere, such as in a disused warehouse, or in a kitchen, bathroom, or garage. Ecstasy is sometimes made in sinks or bathtubs. Often, the people who make it do not know very much about chemistry. Unwanted chemical reactions may take place, and the end product may not even be **MDMA**. It is often a mixture of different **MDA-type drugs**, without any ecstasy at all.

International trade

From the secret laboratories where ecstasy is produced, the drug may be smuggled all over the globe, often by well-organized criminal gangs. Ecstasy enters other countries via the postal service, and by road, sea, and air transport. After this the pills are sold on to users through a network of drug dealers.

Drug dealers

Drug dealers may sell ecstasy from their home, or they may deliver the drugs to the homes of

I A Canadian police officer guards a huge stash of ecstasy pills and a large amount of cash, seized during a police raid on an illegal ecstasy laboratory.

worried. They are not doing this to be kind or helpful – their main aim is to sell as many drugs as possible. They are in a business, and they want to make money.

Friends of users

It is thought that more than half of the people who use ecstasy obtain the drug from friends or other people they know, rather than from a dealer. Even if no money changes hands, giving drugs to a friend is a crime. Friends are often ignorant of the real dangers of drugs. They may give the wrong information, or not know what to do if something goes wrong.

It's impossible to tell what is in an ecstasy pill by looking at it. Many of the pills and capsules sold as ecstasy contain different amounts of **MDMA**, so their effects are unpredictable. Sometimes they contain no MDMA at all, but contain dangerous combinations of other drugs.

▌Dealers will sell almost anything to make a profit, even if it is fake or dangerous. Some people have ended up swallowing chemicals that are used to clean fish tanks, thinking they were taking ecstasy.

■ Ecstasy is sometimes sold in the form of MDMA powder, which is made up of tiny crystals. It may be much stronger than people expect, so it is easy to take too much by accident.

Street drugs today

One reason illegal drugs are so harmful is because people do not know what they are buying. Over the last few years, individual ecstasy pills have tended to contain less and less MDMA. Many other cheap ingredients are used to bulk the drug out, to make a bigger profit for drug **dealers**.

Ecstasy pills may contain a mixture of other drugs, or they may be fakes that have no mind-altering effects at all. Pills may contain other street drugs, such as **ketamine**, **LSD** (acid), **amphetamines** (speed), or less well-known drugs. These can all have dangerous side effects. Some dealers have even been caught selling dog-worming tablets or fish tank cleaner as ecstasy.

Viewpoints

Some nightclubs in the Netherlands offer a drug testing service, allowing ecstasy users to get an idea of what is in their pills before they decide whether to take them. Some people think this is a good idea, but others disagree with this policy.

● **Testing drugs allows users to get a better idea of what is in the pills**
Many pills sold as ecstasy today are fakes. If the pills are found to have no MDMA in them, or to contain other drugs, users can decide not to take them. These tests might stop someone taking substances, or combinations of substances, that are even more harmful than ecstasy.

● **Testing drugs gives a false sense of safety and sends out the wrong message**
The kits used to test drugs are not 100 per cent reliable. They don't say how much MDMA is in a tablet, so users could take much more than they expected to. The tests cannot warn about any poisons the drugs might contain. Testing drugs in nightclubs sends a message that it is OK to take ecstasy, even though it is illegal, and it has many health risks.

What do you think?

Ecstasy affects individual people differently, but the drug usually takes effect 20 to 60 minutes after it has been taken. When these effects wear off, the user experiences an unpleasant "**comedown**".

The first effects of ecstasy

The first effects are sometimes called "coming up". People often get panicky feelings, a sensation of "butterflies in the stomach", or they may vomit. The jaw usually tightens, and the person may begin to sweat and get a dry throat and mouth. After this, the drug takes full effect, which is sometimes called "rolling", or being "up" or "pilled up". Users say they feel more energetic, and that if there is music playing they want to dance to it for hours. Their senses may be heightened, so they may start to enjoy types of music they didn't like before. Many ecstasy users say they have a sensation of **empathy** and closeness towards the people around them.

! Mixing ecstasy with alcohol

Taking ecstasy can lead to dehydration (see pages 28–29), which can be made worse by dancing for long periods in overheated clubs. Alcohol also causes dehydration, so the combination of ecstasy and alcohol is particularly dangerous.

Other effects may include:

- uncontrollable grinding of the jaw and face pulling ("gurning")
- dilated pupils, shaky movements, and muscle cramps
- feelings of anxiety or confusion
- repeating movements over and over again, such as shaking the head.

The effects of ecstasy can vary greatly from person to person. They depend on the amount of the drug that has been taken, how recently the person has eaten a meal, the person's body size and weight, and whether they've taken the drug before. The person's mood and overall health can also make a

Question

How long do the effects of ecstasy last?

difference – for example, if someone is feeling anxious or generally unwell, they may end up feeling much worse.

When ecstasy takes effect, it affects a person's senses, appearance, and behaviour.

Effects on the body

Ecstasy's powerful effects on the chemistry of the brain lead to changes in the body, such as a higher body temperature, increased **blood pressure**, **dehydration**, and a reduced sense of thirst. The physical changes can have dangerous results, even on people who think they're fit and healthy. In some cases, they have led to collapse or even death.

Answer

The initial effects of ecstasy may last from four to six hours, but the after-effects may last for days (see pages 24–25).

Up for hours, down for days

A few hours after someone has taken ecstasy, the effects start to wear off and the person starts to feel exhausted and miserable. This experience is sometimes called a "**comedown**". It always happens to some degree, and it's always unpleasant. While the first effects of ecstasy may last up to 6 hours, the effects of a comedown last at least 24 hours, and may continue for three or four days.

What causes a comedown?

As we have seen, when someone takes ecstasy it causes a sudden release of chemicals such as **serotonin** in the brain. By the time the effects of ecstasy wear off, the amount of these chemicals in some parts of the brain has dropped to a very low level. This chemical imbalance in the brain can leave a user feeling very tired. At the same time, they may also be feeling exhausted from too much physical activity and lack of sleep. If somebody has been dancing all night, they may have pushed their body beyond its normal limits. A comedown from ecstasy can also make people with mental health problems, such as depression or anxiety, feel much worse.

"I know if my boyfriend's taken pills the day before. He's so moody I can't stand to be around him, and he says the nastiest things. I'm not going to put up with it much longer."

Kate, aged sixteen

What does a comedown feel like?

The feelings people have during a comedown from ecstasy vary from person to person. However, many people experience the following:

- exhaustion and a need to sleep for a long time
- feelings of irritation and being bad tempered or "snappy"
- mood swings
- anxiety or **paranoia** (feeling people are "out to get you")
- difficulty concentrating at school, at work, or in other situations.

Many ecstasy users think they can make up for the strain ecstasy has placed on their body by taking vitamins or herbal supplements, or by eating fruits or special foods. While this can help ease the feelings a little, it cannot truly get rid of the comedown. You can't use the body like a bank account, draining it one day, and trying to put things back another day – your body simply doesn't work like that.

❙ It's very common for users to feel very tired, restless, or unhappy for two or more days after taking ecstasy.

There are many serious health risks that come with taking ecstasy. Users are at risk of **heat stroke**, **dehydration**, and **overhydration**. Ecstasy can also cause heart failure and **seizures** (convulsions or fits). It is not just regular users who are at risk. Even a single ecstasy tablet can lead to death.

Ecstasy and body heat

Taking ecstasy raises the body temperature. It also encourages users to dance energetically for long periods, which makes them feel even hotter. Many nightclubs are very hot and crowded, making it difficult to cool down. These factors may combine to cause users to become overheated, and in some cases they may suffer from heat stroke.

❚ People who dance energetically for long periods on hot dance floors are advised to take regular breaks from dancing, to help them cool down. This is true whether they have taken ecstasy or not.

The dangers of heat stroke

Heat stroke is a very dangerous condition in which the body temperature becomes too high. In severe cases of heat stroke, the body temperature rises to over 40 °C and a person may have seizures. The heat can also damage cells all over the body, and cause fatal swelling of the brain, or bleeding into the brain. Bleeding into the brain, sometimes called a **brain haemorrhage** or **stroke**, can cause **paralysis** or death.

Signs of heat stroke

The signs of heat stroke vary but can include:

■ an extremely high body temperature

■ red, hot, and dry skin, often with no sweating

■ rapid, strong **pulse**

■ throbbing headache

■ dizziness

■ **nausea** and vomiting

■ confusion or unconsciousness.

If you see any of these signs in someone who has taken ecstasy, call for medical help immediately, and help the person to cool down. Do not give them alcoholic drinks.

Mike's story

Mike thought it was going to be another ordinary night out with his friends. They had been out for a couple of hours when one of his friends started to feel ill. He had taken ecstasy earlier in the night.

"I was horrified when my friend collapsed on the dance floor and started thrashing around. By the time the medics appeared, his body lay completely still. His eyes were wide open and lifeless when they carried him off on a stretcher."

Fortunately, the paramedics were able to revive Mike's friend, and they took him to hospital. Mike was scared about telling them that his friend had taken ecstasy, but they reassured him that he had done the right thing, and may have saved his friend's life.

Ecstasy and dehydration

The amount of water in the body is very important. In a healthy person, water makes up around 70 per cent of the whole weight of the body. It also makes up about 90 per cent of the volume of the blood. **Dehydration** occurs when someone loses water and important blood salts from the body, often through heavy sweating. This can be very dangerous and can happen after losing only a small amount of water and salts from the body.

Question

What are the signs of ecstasy dehydration?

Ecstasy can cause dehydration because it raises a person's body temperature and causes them to sweat a lot. Hot dance floors and dancing for a long time make users sweat even more, making dehydration worse. The drug also reduces the sensations of tiredness and thirst in many people, so the body's natural warning signs of dehydration may be missed or ignored.

Why is dehydration dangerous?

Once the level of water and salt in the body drops below a certain level, vital organs, such as the kidneys, brain, and heart, cannot function properly. Cramps may develop and **blood pressure** may become dangerously low. Severe cases of dehydration can lead to **hallucinations**, the collapse of the **circulatory system** (heart and blood vessels), and death.

If you think somebody is dehydrated, help them away from hot areas and call for medical help. Encourage them to sit down and slowly sip up to half a pint of water, but no more. Do not give them anything containing alcohol, or drinks containing caffeine such as cola or coffee. These drinks will make them even more dehydrated.

Too much fluid

Many ecstasy users drink lots of water to avoid dehydration, but drinking too much water can also be very harmful. This is because ecstasy causes the kidneys to stop working normally. Instead of being expelled from the body in the urine, excess water is retained in the body. This can lead to **overhydration**. Symptoms of overhydration include confusion, dizziness, a fast heart or breathing rate, and **seizures**. Overhydration can also cause dangerous swelling of the brain, which can lead to death.

❙ The body's fluid and salt levels are in a delicate balance. Some ecstasy users have collapsed after drinking too much water, and others have collapsed after drinking too little water.

Answer

Early signs include passing small amounts of dark urine or no urine at all, flushed skin, and light-headedness. Later signs include severe confusion, rapid breathing, a weak **pulse**, shrivelled skin, sunken eyes, pain when passing urine, clumsiness, and leg cramps.

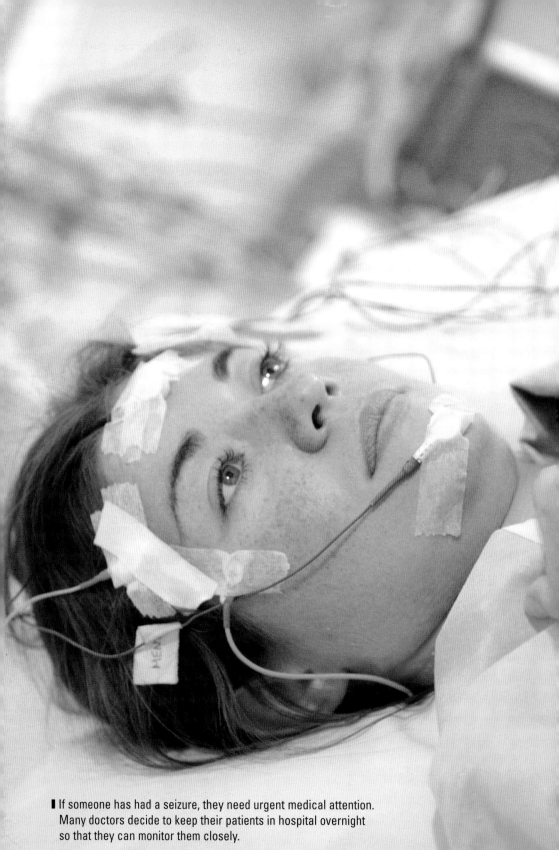

▌If someone has had a seizure, they need urgent medical attention. Many doctors decide to keep their patients in hospital overnight so that they can monitor them closely.

Heart failure

Ecstasy causes massive increases in the heart rate, and in the force at which the heart pumps blood around the body. Some people who have taken ecstasy have died from the heart being unable to cope with this extra strain on the **circulatory system**. It is possible that some of these people were suffering from heart problems that had previously been unnoticed. They may have been born with a problem, and may have felt perfectly healthy all their lives until they took ecstasy.

Ecstasy and seizures

Ecstasy has also been shown to cause **seizures**. Like all **stimulant** drugs, ecstasy increases the activity between the nerve cells of the brain. This increased nerve cell activity can cause fits in ecstasy users who have **epilepsy**. Ecstasy has also caused seizures in people who do not have epilepsy.

When someone suffers a seizure, they lose consciousness and fall to the ground. Their muscles become rigid or tense, their face may turn blue, and their body starts shaking. Most commonly, the shaking lasts for a minute or two, after which the person regains some consciousness, often feeling confused and wanting sleep.

! The risks of other club drugs

- **Amphetamines** (also called speed) – these are stimulant drugs that make users feel alert and awake. They can be **addictive** and cause many health problems.

- **Ketamine** (also called K, special K) – this is a powerful drug that is used to make animals unconscious during surgery. Ketamine can cause **hallucinations** and make users feel completely disorientated. The drug also causes **nausea**, vomiting, and blackouts. It is especially dangerous if mixed with alcohol or other drugs.

- **Rohypnol** (also called roofies) – this is a **sedative** drug that makes people feel sleepy. Recently, there have been cases of rape involving the use of this drug. Attackers slip the drug into a person's food or drink without their knowing (this is known as "spiking"). The victim becomes very drowsy or even unconscious, so they are helpless and vulnerable to attack.

- **GHB** (also called liquid ecstasy) – this is a sedative drug that makes people feel drunk or sleepy. It can cause fits, **coma**, or death and has also been used to make people unable to defend themselves against sexual attack.

- **Amyl and butyl nitrites** (also called poppers) – when inhaled, these cause a "head rush" and make the heart pound. Users may pass out or have terrible headaches. Nitrites can also cause heart attacks in some people, and rashes on the face.

Other health risks

Ecstasy can cause a number of other health problems,
including wear and tear on the body and organ damage.
Some of these health problems are more common than others.

Many ecstasy users experience:

- injuries from over-exercising, such as back pain, sprains,
  and sore muscles
- mouth ulcers, worn teeth, cracked tooth enamel, and
  pains in the jaw, caused by tooth grinding
- rashes on the face and neck, and increased acne breakouts.

In some cases users may suffer from kidney
failure, liver damage, and heart problems.

Ecstasy may also cause existing health
problems to become worse, including asthma,
epilepsy, high **blood pressure**, depression,
and anxiety.

❚ Ecstasy users seem to be
at greater risk of catching
colds and flu than people
who do not use the drug.
The reason for this is
unknown.

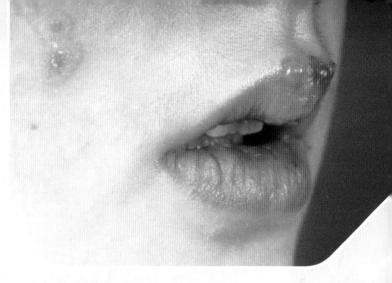

■ The virus that causes **cold sores** may be reactivated if someone becomes run down after staying up all night and taking drugs.

Ecstasy and the immune system

The **immune system** exists to fight off infections caused by bacteria and viruses. Ecstasy use may make the immune system less effective, meaning that users are more likely to suffer from colds and flu than other people. Being run down after using ecstasy may also lead to the return of certain viruses that may be "dormant" or inactive in the body. This may be a direct effect of the drug, or it may be caused by staying up late and doing too much energetic dancing and then not sleeping or eating properly for a while. Top athletes who want to stay in peak condition are always careful not to over-exercise – they know it isn't good for their overall health or performance.

Changes in behaviour

Taking ecstasy can make a difference to the way people behave. While they are under the influence of the drug, they may say or do things they later regret. For example, users may become very chatty and tell people very personal things about themselves. They may later wish they had kept that information private. Ecstasy can also affect a person's ability to make sensible, responsible decisions. This can lead to people having accidents or being attacked physically or sexually. Users may also have unprotected sex, putting themselves at risk of unwanted pregnancy or **sexually transmitted infections (STIs)**, or they may sleep with someone they wouldn't normally like or trust.

⚠ Ecstasy and pregnancy

Taking any drug during pregnancy is very risky. Some experts believe taking ecstasy during pregnancy can lead to babies being born with birth defects.

Many ecstasy users say that the drug is safe, but there is no doubt that ecstasy can kill. Some of the biggest killers in ecstasy users are **heat stroke**, **overhydration**, and heart failure. It's impossible to guess who is likely to die, and even one pill can have a deadly effect.

Facts, not myths

A number of people have died as a direct result of taking ecstasy. Most of these people appeared to be completely healthy before taking the drug. When people die from ecstasy use, it's common for other users to say it was a "bad" or poisoned pill, or that the person who took the drug didn't behave correctly and died because of their mistake. The truth is that most of these deaths were simply a reaction to taking ecstasy.

❚ Although many ecstasy users say that they are not hurting anyone, if they become ill or die their relatives and friends suffer a traumatic experience.

■ Ecstasy-related illness and deaths

- Between 1997 and 2002 there were 200 ecstasy-related deaths in England and Wales, and in a similar period there were 73 deaths in Scotland.

- In the United States in 2002, ecstasy use led to 4,026 hospital emergency department visits. Ecstasy kills over 40 people each year in the United States.

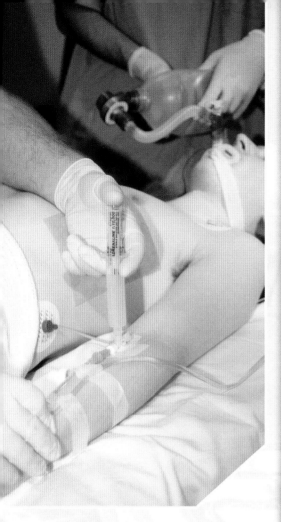

| Taking a single ecstasy pill can lead to a severe and unexpected reaction, even when the pill is not contaminated with other harmful drugs.

Ecstasy overdoses

The risks of death after taking ecstasy are increased if someone takes a large amount of the drug. Because the amount of **MDMA** varies from pill to pill, users may accidentally take more than their body can cope with (an **overdose**). Taking ecstasy in combination with other drugs increases the risk of an overdose.

Viewpoints

In some nightclubs ecstasy users are told to drink water, avoid alcoholic drinks, and take breaks from dancing. This approach is sometimes referred to as "harm reduction" because it may reduce the risks involved in taking ecstasy. Some people think that this approach is a good idea. Others disagree.

- **Harm reduction saves lives**
  You can't stop people taking ecstasy, so it's a good idea to reduce some of its risks. A harm reduction approach decreases the risk of **dehydration** and heat stroke, which are both big killers.

- **Harm reduction encourages people to take more drugs**
  Harm reduction gives people a false impression that ecstasy is a "safe" drug. It sends out the wrong message and might make ecstasy seem attractive to people who would not try it otherwise. Dehydration and heat stroke are only two of the risks of taking ecstasy. Drinking too much water can also kill, and harm reduction does not prevent that.

What do you think?

Ecstasy is not physically **addictive** in the same way as some other drugs, such as heroin. But some people may develop an ecstasy habit they find hard to give up.

Addiction and tolerance

When someone becomes physically addicted to a drug, it causes changes in the user's body, which make their body need the drug in order to function. The person's body becomes so used to taking the drug that when they stop taking it, they become physically ill. This is what happens when people become addicted to heroin. The same effect does not appear to happen with ecstasy. However, a person who takes ecstasy regularly builds up a **tolerance** to the drug as their body requires larger and larger doses of the drug in order to experience the same effects.

▌ After a period of regular ecstasy use, people have to take more and more of the drug to get the same effect. Using more each time means there's a greater chance of taking more than the body can cope with.

Psychological dependence

Psychological dependence happens when people use drugs to get through everyday life, and feel that they cannot cope without them. Although most people who try ecstasy do not become psychologically dependent on it, some regular users do develop dependence. Dependence can build up slowly, and may be quite unexpected. Compared to users of many other street drugs, the people who become dependent on ecstasy tend to be quite young.

Signs of dependence

Early signs of ecstasy dependence may include a person:

- spending long periods thinking about ecstasy, getting hold of the drug, or taking the drug
- feeling that they need ecstasy just to get through the week, or to cope with social events
- becoming angry when someone challenges them about their ecstasy use
- having sudden changes in moods or behaviour
- missing lots of school or work
- spending less time on their usual interests.

It's important to remember that some of these signs have other causes, and do not necessarily mean someone has developed dependence on ecstasy.

"It's like you need more of it just to keep you happy. It was affecting my brain and its normal thought patterns. I was losing myself quick and could hardly remember the little things I used to do that made me happy and made me feel comfortable to be me. I was nothing but a drug addict."

Josh, aged seventeen, who recently gave up taking ecstasy

Like any drug that changes a person's emotional state, ecstasy can cause mood swings and other mental health problems. It may also cause anxiety, **panic attacks**, depression, **paranoia**, and memory problems in some users. These effects may last for many months in some people.

▋ If you are with someone who is suffering from anxiety or panic, lead them away from loud noises, bright lights, and crowded areas. If they do not feel calmer after a few minutes of sitting quietly, ask someone to get help from nearby first-aiders or from paramedics.

Short-term anxiety

As we have already seen, it's common for users to feel anxious or panicky for a few minutes after ecstasy first takes effect. In some people these feelings of panic may continue for hours. This is most likely to happen if someone takes ecstasy when they are feeling upset and worried. However, even people who are relaxed when they take the drug may experience these negative feelings. The **comedown** that begins as ecstasy wears off can also make people feel stressed out and anxious, often for days.

Long-term anxiety

Experts believe that even the smallest amount of ecstasy can cause long-term anxiety problems. They have found this out by studying the effects of the drug on animals. In a number of different experiments, rats and mice were given ecstasy and they showed signs of anxious behaviour for months afterwards. This may be linked with decreased levels of **serotonin** in their brains (see pages 8–9). Although humans were not used in these experiments, there is increasing evidence that regular ecstasy users may end up with serious anxiety problems, even years after giving the drugs up.

Nick's story

Nick first took ecstasy at a party with friends, and started using it every time he went out to nightclubs. He soon found that one pill was not having much of an effect, and started to take more. The dose was unpredictable. Sometimes he took much more than he wanted to and felt anxious and paranoid.

"As my use of the drug increased, so did the unpredictable effects and the feelings of panic, both at the time and for days afterwards. One evening I took two pills that were stronger than anything I'd had before. Everyone on the dance floor looked frightening to me, staring at me with dark hollow eyes. For the rest of the week dark emotions, highlighted by self-loathing and severe anxiety, crashed down on me."

Although Nick was scared to admit how he was feeling, he eventually confided in his girlfriend, and realized that it was time to stop taking ecstasy for good.

Memory problems and brain damage

As their research continues, scientists are discovering more about ecstasy-related brain damage. Evidence from tests suggests that ecstasy users are more likely to have problems with learning and remembering things, compared with people who do not use ecstasy.

■ There are times when we all need to be able to concentrate properly, and to rely on our memories. Research suggests that even a small amount of ecstasy can affect a person's ability to remember things.

Memory problems can be detected even months after someone has used ecstasy. Some researchers think that the drug can harm the part of the brain that is responsible for making decisions and using judgement. The brain damage that ecstasy seems to cause may not be completely reversible, especially in heavy users.

Ecstasy and depression

Use of ecstasy can make people feel down and miserable for long periods. It may also make someone feel as if they can't be bothered with anything. In animal studies, ecstasy causes signs of long-term depression. Experts believe ecstasy affects humans in the same way, especially if large doses have been taken. Users may lose their sense of enjoyment in things they used to love. They may also have problems with sleep and appetite. It is quite common for depressed people to become much less sociable, and they may lose contact with many of the people they know. Someone who is depressed may even have thoughts of suicide.

Ecstasy and paranoia

Using ecstasy can increase the risk of a person becoming **paranoid**. If someone is paranoid, they often think that somebody or something is trying to harm them, even though this isn't true. For example, they may wrongly think people want to attack them or poison them, or that they are being followed or watched. They may also worry that they have a terrible illness, or that their friends are talking about them behind their back. Paranoid thoughts can lead to arguments or physical violence.

Ecstasy and psychosis

Psychosis is a severe mental disorder in which a person loses contact with reality and cannot function properly in normal life. This can happen if a person is suffering from an illness such as **schizophrenia**. It can also happen to people after taking ecstasy.

❚ Most people who suffer from depression need to see a doctor, and may need **counselling**, **therapy**, or medication.

❗ Personality changes

Ecstasy use may affect a user's personality. Experts do not know whether this is a direct effect of the drug, or whether it results from changes in the user's lifestyle and friendship groups.

41

Taking drugs such as ecstasy can have harmful effects on a person's health, but it can also damage their education, their relationships, and their prospects in life. Drug use also causes distress and problems for others, including family, friends, and the many people in society who have to deal with the problems associated with drug use.

Damaged lives

As we have seen, in spite of what many users may say, ecstasy has not been proven to be a "safe" drug. Everyone thinks "it won't happen to me", but some people are wrong about this every year, and have their lives cut short unexpectedly. Many others have ended up in hospital.

▌Anyone who knows an ecstasy user may have to cope with a person who is suffering from mood swings and extreme tiredness. This can be very stressful and lead to family arguments.

■ Travellers are often required to show a visa at passport control before they can enter another country. Many countries refuse to issue visas to people who have been convicted of a drug offence.

Ecstasy can damage a person's life in many other ways. Ecstasy can affect a person's ability to concentrate and remember what they have learnt. This can seriously affect a person's performance at school. They may do badly in some key exams, which may stop them from getting on a course they were aiming for. A conviction for a drug offence can land a young person in jail. It can also prevent them from achieving their goals in life, stand between them and their chosen career, and prevent them from travelling abroad. Heavy drug users may find that they drift away from their social group and lose some of their oldest friends. They may also lose their jobs, which can lead to money problems.

Who else suffers?

Some people who take drugs say they aren't hurting anyone but themselves. However, when someone has a problem with drugs, many other people suffer too. Bad-tempered drug users can be hard to deal with, and may say hurtful things to the people they care about, placing a strain on relationships.

"I know my son uses ecstasy. I've tried to talk to him about it, to get him to stop. He lies about his drug use and stays out all night, and then goes for days without smiling or being his usual self. The rest of the family are walking on eggshells around him when he gets bad tempered, which is often. He can't see how he's behaving, or admit it."

Kathleen, mother of an ecstasy user

Costs to society

Drug abuse, including ecstasy abuse, affects the whole of society. People who use ecstasy often need to take time off work because of the after-effects of the drug or they may not be able to do their jobs so effectively. This affects the company they work for, and also puts a strain on people they work with.

Medical care

Every year, many people need emergency medical care after taking ecstasy. Busy paramedics, doctors, and nurses all have to work hard to care for these people. Some users also need long-term treatment for depression and other mental health problems they suffer after using ecstasy. This can result in years of expensive medical care or **counselling**. All of these problems take doctors and other health professionals away from their work with other patients.

■ If someone becomes ill after taking drugs such as ecstasy, medical staff not only have to treat them, they also have the added strain of breaking bad news to the person's family.

As we have seen, some experts believe that babies born to women who take ecstasy while they are pregnant are more likely to be born with birth defects. These babies need extra healthcare at birth, and they may also need long-term health and social care. These healthcare costs have to be paid for by individuals, governments, or insurance companies.

The costs of crime

Governments all around the world spend vast sums of money on preventing the production, **supply**, and use of illegal drugs. Along with other illegal drugs, ecstasy is linked to the actions of criminal gangs, which make huge profits from the trade in illegal drugs. Some of the money from illegal drug sales may even end up funding **terrorism**.

Drug crimes also affect people who have nothing to do with drug use. Some people are killed in accidents caused by people who take drugs and then drive. Ecstasy seriously impairs a person's ability to drive a vehicle, even though they may feel confident about their driving. Innocent people can be robbed, attacked, and threatened by drug **dealers** or people who are under the influence of drugs. Tackling the crimes associated with drugs takes up the valuable time and resources of the police, the courts, and the prison system.

Costs to the individual

Everyone has to pay for the problems associated with illegal drug use. Individuals have to pay for the extra work done by the police, customs officers, and medical professionals through higher taxes or increased insurance premiums. Some people argue that this money would be better spent on other things, such as better education about drugs.

❚ Detecting and arresting drug dealers and drug users, as well as filling in the related paperwork, takes up an enormous amount of police time.

Ecstasy and the law

Ecstasy is an illegal drug – it is illegal to make it, sell it, possess it, and use it. All of these crimes carry strict penalties. Being ignorant about the law is not an excuse that can be given in court. A criminal record for a drug offence can affect a person's chances of getting a good job or going to college.

Possession

If someone has control over any amount of a drug, including ecstasy, this is called **possession**. This could mean that a person is carrying a small amount of the drug, or is keeping the drugs in a certain place, such as a locker or a bedroom drawer. If someone is caught with a large amount of ecstasy, the police may assume that it is not for their own personal use, and may charge them with possession with "intent to **supply**". In other words, they can be accused of being a drug **dealer**, and face much tougher punishment.

Trafficking

Transporting or smuggling ecstasy between different states or countries is called **trafficking**, and can lead to long prison sentences. This offence is taken much more seriously than possession, and large amounts of drugs are usually involved. Trafficking can lead to very heavy fines and life in prison.

❗ Supplying drugs

Supply means giving or selling drugs to other people. It doesn't just apply to drug dealers who make money from selling ecstasy. Giving away a single pill for free to a friend can get someone arrested for supply. Looking after some drugs for a friend can also get a person arrested for supply when they give the drugs back.

❚ Customs officers and specially trained sniffer dogs check luggage at airports to prevent drug smuggling.

Punishment for drug crimes

Ecstasy has been banned in the United Kingdom since 1977. It is a Class A drug, along with cocaine and heroin. There are serious penalties for possession – up to seven years in prison plus an unlimited fine. Supplying ecstasy can lead to a life sentence. In Australia, federal, state, and territory laws exist for possessing, using, making, and selling the drug. The punishment depends on the amount of ecstasy involved, but fines are usually heavy and a prison sentence is a possibility. In New Zealand, ecstasy is a Class B2 drug, although some people are calling for it to be reclassed as a B1 drug with harsher penalties.

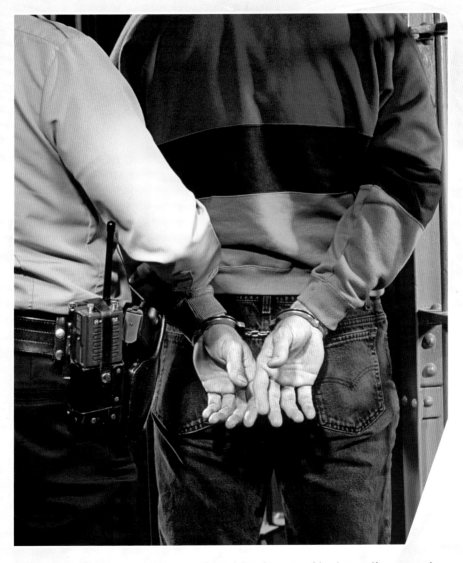

❚ Did you know that you can be arrested for giving drugs to a friend, even if no money is involved? It is illegal, and ignorance is no excuse.

There are many reasons why people decide to give up ecstasy. Most users are able to give up on their own without help, but there is plenty of help and advice available for people who find it more of a struggle.

Deciding to give up

Many users say they want to stop using ecstasy because they are worried about the health risks of the drug, or the effect that it's having on their mind. They may have suffered unpleasant **comedowns**, or feelings of anxiety and panic. They may be having problems concentrating or remembering things at school or work. They might have important exams coming up, and feel that they want to do their best.

Sometimes people decide to stop when their personal situation changes. They might be starting a new relationship, and feel that they don't need to take ecstasy any more. They might be starting

❚ Talking things through in confidence with a trained drug **counsellor** can be a helpful way to break unhealthy behaviour patterns for good.

a new job and need to be more alert every day. Some people say they get bored with the club scene, or that they want room in their lives for other interests.

Seeking help

Most ecstasy users give up without needing any professional help. Studies suggest that less than 1 per cent of ecstasy users seek help when they are trying to give up the drug. However, some people who are being treated for **addiction** to other drugs also have a problem with ecstasy. If someone does have a problem giving up ecstasy, it can be useful to seek medical advice.

Treatment may involve **therapy**, **counselling**, and medical help for mental health problems caused by the drug, such as depression. Some users find it helpful to join groups of ex-users for moral support, or go to group therapy.

❙ Ecstasy use can seriously get in the way of having a healthy lifestyle. That's one reason why so many users decide to give up.

Billy's story

Billy, aged twenty, says taking ecstasy almost made him lose his job. He has now given up ecstasy completely.

"I stopped taking pills because I was having **panic attacks**, and my comedowns were getting worse. I spent more time coming down than I did feeling straight. My idea of a good weekend involved at least ten pills. I finally gave up when, one day, I was talking to my boss and I suddenly gripped the desk in a panic because I felt as if I'd fallen off a cliff. I hadn't fallen. I was on the ground floor. It was a long time before I started to feel OK again."

Are there things that worry you about ecstasy? If there are – either now or in the future – there are lots of people you can contact. There are many organizations that offer help and advice on ecstasy and ecstasy-related problems. You can find out more information about these organizations on pages 54–55 of this book.

Getting the best advice

If you're looking for advice about ecstasy or other drugs, you have to be choosy about where you start looking. Friends, relatives, and other people you meet may mean well, but they don't always know the truth about drugs. Drug **dealers** are mainly interested in making money, not in making sure people are safe, so you can't trust anything they say. There are several organizations that provide reliable information about drugs, and many of them run confidential helplines that can give you advice about ecstasy. You can also pick up leaflets and books at your local school, college, or library.

❗ Coping with pressure

One day, you may be offered drugs by someone you know or by a dealer. It's a good idea to think ahead about how you're going to react. It's important to remember:

- taking drugs does not make someone "cool"
- taking ecstasy has many health risks
- whatever people say, it's OK to say "no" to drugs.

If you're offered drugs you can:

- say "no" or "no thanks"
- give a reason why you don't want to take drugs
- walk away from the person.

Most of all, remember – it's your life. Nobody else can tell you what to do. It's up to you to make your own decisions.

❚ Good friends will respect your decisions, whether about drugs or anything else in your life.

Someone to talk to

If you want to ask questions or have a general chat in confidence, your school or college may have somebody you can talk to, such as a school nurse or a **counsellor**. You can also talk to a drugs helpline operator, or see your family doctor. They will be able to put you in touch with the right kind of help, and anything you say will be kept completely private.

Worried about someone else?

A number of groups and charities have been set up to give support and advice to anyone who has a friend, partner, or relative with a drugs problem. If you're worried about someone else's drug use, don't feel that you have to bottle all your feelings up and try to cope with something like this on your own.

Glossary

abuse use of drugs for non-medical reasons in a way that has a bad effect

addiction when a person is dependent on (unable to manage without) a drug and finds it extremely hard to stop using it

amphetamine type of stimulant drug that speeds up the activity of the brain. Amphetamines are often added to tablets sold as ecstasy. They can cause severe addiction and many health problems.

amyl and butyl nitrites street drugs that are inhaled to give a "head rush". They can cause rashes on the face or heart attacks in some people, and are poisonous if swallowed.

blood pressure pressure of the blood as it circulates around the body

brain haemorrhage bleeding into the tissues of the brain

circulatory system system made up of the heart and blood vessels, which allows blood to move around the body continuously

cold sore inflamed blister in or near the mouth, caused by a virus

coma state of deep unconsciousness from which it is very hard or even impossible to wake a person

comedown feelings of tiredness experienced as the effects of a drug wear off, caused by a chemical imbalance in the brain

counselling advice and guidance given to people to help resolve their problems

counsellor person trained to give advice and guidance to people to help resolve their problems

dealer person who buys and sells drugs illegally

dehydration loss of essential fluids from the body

empathy ability to understand and share someone else's feelings

epilepsy medical condition in which a person has sudden attacks of altered sensation, loss of consciousness, or seizures

GHB shortened name of Gammahydroxybutyrate, a drug that makes users feel drunk or sleepy. It can cause seizures, coma, and death.

hallucination experience of seeing or hearing something that is not really present and only exists in the mind

hallucinogen substance that distorts the way a person sees and feels things, and causes hallucinations

heat stroke medical condition caused by the failure of the body's natural temperature regulation system

hippy person who is opposed to many of the accepted ideas about how to live and dress. Hippies often have long hair. They are particularly associated with the 1960s and the taking of hallucinogenic drugs.

immune system the body's natural defence against infection

ketamine synthetic anaesthetic drug that can cause frightening hallucinations, vomiting, and unconsciousness

LSD drug that can cause strong hallucinations. It is also known as "acid".

MDA-type drugs large group of drugs, including ecstasy, that have both stimulant and hallucinogenic effects

MDMA MDMA is the chemical name for ecstasy. It is short for 3, 4-methylenedioxymethamphetamine.

nausea feeling of sickness and need to vomit

overdose excessive dose of a drug, which the body cannot cope with

overhydration condition in which excess water is retained in the body

panic attack sudden very strong feeling of anxiety, which makes a person's heart race

paralysis loss of the ability to move part or all of the body

paranoia mental condition involving feelings of suspicion and distrust – a sense that everyone is "out to get you", or to criticize your behaviour or actions

possession owning or having an illegal drug (either carrying it or having it hidden somewhere)

psychological connected with the mind, for example feelings and moods

psychological dependence when a person feels they need drugs to get through everyday life and cannot cope without them

pulse rhythmic throbbing of the arteries as the heart pumps blood through them

raves all-night parties, often staged illegally, where dance music is played

Rohypnol strong sedative drug that makes people very drowsy

schizophrenia serious mental disorder that can lead to confused thinking and changes in a person's personality and behaviour

sedative drug that causes someone to become calm or sleepy

seizure sudden attack that causes the body to go into spasm (also known as a fit or convulsion)

serotonin messenger chemical in the brain that seems to be important for the control of moods, emotions, and eating and sleeping patterns

sexually transmitted infection (STI) infection that is spread through sexual activity

stimulant drug that speeds up the activity of the brain, making people feel alert and full of energy

stroke sudden change in the blood supply to part of the brain, which can cause loss of physical functions such as movement or speech

supply give or sell drugs to other people

synthetic made artificially using chemicals

terrorism use of violence or intimidation in the hope of achieving a political aim

therapy treatment that helps someone to get better. Therapy often involves talking.

tolerance need for larger and larger doses of a drug to get the same effect

trafficking smuggling or transporting drugs, usually in large amounts

Contacts and further information

There are a number of organizations that provide information and advice about drugs. Some have helpful websites, or provide information packs and leaflets, while others offer help and support over the phone.

Contacts in the UK

Adfam
Waterbridge House, 32–36 Loman Street, London SE1 0EH
Tel: 020 7928 8898
www.adfam.org.uk
Adfam is a national charity that gives confidential support and information to the families and friends of drug users. They also run family-support groups.

Childline
Helpline: 0800 1111
A 24-hour number for any young person in distress to call. Offers confidential help and guidance from trained counsellors on a range of issues, including family problems caused by drugs.

Connexions Direct
Helpline: 080 800 13219
(8 a.m.–2 a.m. daily)
Text: 07766 4 13219
www.connexions-direct.com
This service for young people aged from thirteen to nineteen offers information and advice on a wide range of topics, including drugs. Young people can also speak to an adviser by telephone, webchat, email, or text message.

DrugScope
32–36 Loman Street, London SE1 0EE
Tel: 020 7928 1211
www.drugscope.org.uk
A national drugs information agency with services that include a library, a wide range of publications, and a website.

Families Anonymous
Doddington & Rollo Community Association, Charlotte Despard Avenue, Battersea, London SW11 5HD
Helpline: 0845 1200 660
www.famanon.org.uk
An organization involved in support groups for parents and families of drug users. They can put you in touch with groups in different parts of the country.

FRANK
Tel: 0800 776600
Email: frank@talktofrank.com
www.talktofrank.com
An organization for young people that gives free, confidential advice and information about drugs 24 hours a day.

Narcotics Anonymous
UK Service Office, 202 City Road, London EC1V 2PH
Helpline: 020 7730 0009
(10 a.m.–10 p.m. daily)
www.ukna.org
A fellowship of people who have given up narcotics, using a twelve-step programme. They have a helpline for users and their friends and relatives, plus events and meetings around the United Kingdom.

Release
Helpline: 0845 4500 215
(10 a.m.–5.30 p.m. Mon–Fri)
Email: ask@release.org.uk
www.release.org.uk
An organization that provides legal advice to drug users, their families, and friends. The advice is free, professional, and confidential.

Contacts in Australia and New Zealand

Alcohol & Other Drugs Council of Australia (ADCA)
17 Napier Close, Deakin, ACT 2600
Tel: 02 6281 1002
www.adca.org.au
ADCA works with the government and community organizations, to prevent or reduce the harm caused by drugs.

Australian Drug Foundation
409 King Street, West Melbourne, VIC 3003
Tel: 03 9278 8100
www.adf.org.au
An organization that works to prevent and reduce drug problems in the Australian community.

The DARE (Drug Abuse Resistance Education) Foundation of New Zealand
PO Box 50744, Porirua, New Zealand
Tel: 04 238 9550
www.dare.org.nz
An organization that provides drug prevention education programmes.

Foundation for Alcohol and Drug Education (FADE)
9 Anzac Street, PO Box 33–1505, Takapuna, Auckland, New Zealand
Tel: 09 489 1719
www.fade.org.nz
A national organization that provides services throughout the country.

Narcotics Anonymous
Australian Service Office, 1st Floor, 204 King Street, Newtown, NSW 2042
http://na.org.au
National helpline: 1300 652 820
The Australian division of Narcotics Anonymous has helplines plus events and meetings around Australia.

Turning Point
54–62 Gertrude Street, Fitzroy, VIC 3065
www.turningpoint.org.au
Helpline (DirectLine): 1800 888 236
Turning Point provides specialist treatment and support services to people affected by drug use.

Further reading

Dr Miriam Stoppard's Drug Information File: From Alcohol and Tobacco to Ecstasy and Heroin, by Miriam Stoppard (Dorling Kindersley, 1999)

Drugs and You, by Bridget Lawless (Heinemann Library, 2000)

Drugs: The Truth, by Aidan Macfarlane and Ann McPherson (Oxford University Press, 2003)

Health Issues: Drugs, by Sarah Lennard-Brown (Hodder Children's Books, 2004)

Just the Facts: Ecstasy, by Sean Connolly (Heinemann Library, 2000)

Teen Issues: Drugs, by Joanna Watson and Joanna Kedge (Raintree, 2004)

Why Do People Take Drugs?, by Patsy Westcott (Hodder Children's Books, 2000)

Further research

If you want to find out more about problems related to ecstasy, you can search the Internet, using a search engine such as Google. Try using keywords such as:

Ecstasy + health
Club drugs
Ecstasy + harm reduction
Ecstasy + law
Ecstasy + dependence

Disclaimer
All the Internet addresses (URLs) given in this book were valid at the time of going to press. However, owing to the dynamic nature of the Internet, some addresses may have changed or sites may have ceased to exist since publication. While the author, packager, and publishers regret any inconvenience this may cause readers, no responsibility for any such change can be accepted by the author, packager, or publishers.

Index